Love You Can Touch

JANE C. JARRELL
Artwork by *Lila Rose Kennedy*

HARVEST HOUSE PUBLISHERS
EUGENE, OREGON

For Our Daughter, Sarah Allegra Jarrell

Love You Can Touch
Copyright © 1999 by Jane Jarrell
Published by Harvest House Publishers
Eugene, Oregon 97402

Library of Congress Cataloging-in-Publication Data

Jarrell, Jane Cabaniss, 1961–
    Love you can touch / Jane Jarrell ; artwork by Lila Rose Kennedy.
        p.   cm.
    ISBN 0-7369-0159-0
    1. Hospitality—Religious aspects—Christianity. 2. Christian women—Religious life. I. Title
    BV4647.H67J37 1999
    241' .671—dc21
                                                                    99-18850
                                                                    CIP

Artwork designs are reproduced under license from © Arts Uniq' ®, Inc., Cookeville, TN and may not be reproduced without permission. For information regarding art prints featured in this book, please contact:

        Arts Uniq'
        P.O. Box 3085
        Cookeville TN 38502
        800-223-5020

Design and production by Garborg Design Works, Minneapolis, Minnesota

Scripture quotations are from The Living Bible, Copyright © 1971 owned by assignment by Illinois Regional Bank N.A. (as trustee). Used by permission of Tyndale House Publishers, Inc., Wheaton, Illinois 60189. All rights reserved; the Holy Bible, New International Version®. Copyright © 1973, 1978, 1984 by the International Bible Society. Used by permission of Zondervan Publishing House; and the King James Version.

Printed in the United States of America

99 00 01 02 03 04 05 06 07 08 / DC / 10 9 8 7 6 5 4 3 2 1

Contents

How to Share Your Heart

When I was growing up I knew what the tantalizing aroma of a coconut pound cake filling our home meant. Either a family member was celebrating a birthday or a friend was having surgery or a new baby was about to make his or her entrance into our world. In a home where gift giving was a treasured thing, cake baking to mark an "occasion" was a ritual. The same is true in my house today. Whatever the event, happy or sad, it is always a perfect time to offer love you can touch.

Showing love, empathy, and encouragement in today's hectic world is considered by many to be time-consuming, frivolous, and one more item to add to a long and trying to-do list. But if you stop and listen to the quiet whispers of your heart, don't you feel a gentle tugging to share with others and show them that you care? Take a step back and approach your life looking through the eyes of eternity. How can you tangibly show the lasting kind of love? What can you say? How do you say it? What can you do to demonstrate your genuine empathy when someone else is happy or when they are hurting?

We can become messengers of goodwill who help others right in our own homes and neighborhoods. The goal is to become true servants by showing love in both word and deed. Whether we serve our friends, our children, our neighbors, our family members, or strangers, we should keep these words from the Book of Romans in mind: "Love must be sincere…Be devoted to one another in brotherly love. Honor one another above yourselves.…Share with God's people who are in need. Practice hospitality."

This book was written to provide you with suggestions for showing love to big and little hearts. You'll find a user-friendly way to prepare, package, and present your messages of love to children and adults. Each chapter feeds the recipient of your gifts delicious meals to nourish the body and refreshing bits of inspiration to nourish the soul.

I've written this book with your grocery list and pocketbook in mind. Every chapter includes easy-to-follow recipes and inexpensive, quick ideas for packaging your creations. It also includes gift ideas that can be tucked into your preparation with limited hassle. You will find ideas for helping others at home as well as ways to teach your children to encourage others.

How to Use *Love You Can Touch*

Planning always sounds like such a time-consuming and boring thing to do, but it is really vital in pulling off the delivery of foods and the fun of packaging. Planning makes everything easier and more enjoyable. Cooking, packaging, and freezing go much faster when you are organized. For starters, it helps you to remember everything to put in the dish. Before you begin to prepare a recipe, assemble everything you will need from the pantry and refrigerator. That way you won't find out halfway through making the peppermint fudge that you don't have any peppermint extract!

Each chapter focuses on a different event that affects individuals and families and offers suggestions for giving gifts to the people in that particular situation. The chapters, which conclude with easy-to-prepare recipes, are divided into four sections:

Love You Can Touch for Adults

This section offers a gift idea for the adults in the family. The gift is a token of caring to fit the particular situation.

Love You Can Touch for Children

This section offers a gift idea for the family's children.

Menu Ideas and Recipes to Nourish the Heart and Soul

A menu has been created to coincide with each event. The menus are flavorful and use easy-to-find ingredients with simple recipe instructions.

Packaging Panache

Each menu comes with ideas for packaging the food items, either to deliver by car or on foot to your friend's home or to mail across the country.

Tucked in between the chapters you will find:
- 10 great gift giving ideas
- 15 ways to wrap a gift without wrapping paper
- Lunch and munch more for kids
- 5 fabulous meals to freeze
- 10 great ideas for tuck'n love in your husband's lunchbox
- Fabulous food finds

You'll find a variety of approaches for ministering to the needs of others through prayer, food, kind words, and compassionate deeds. It is a guide to helping you truly demonstrate hospitality and actions of brotherly love. And it is also a road map for showing love, sharing love, and teaching love through your actions.

CHAPTER 1

New Neighbor

Love your neighbor.
—The Book of Matthew

Good neighbors are a gift. When someone purchases or rents a home or moves into an apartment, they often plan to live there for many years. They select the location and building—sometimes even designing it themselves! Unfortunately, nobody can select the people who live on either side of them, so if they are good people both neighbors are truly blessed. Extending a warm welcome to a new family is a good way to begin what could easily become a lifelong friendship. A strong neighborhood is an extension of the home, from the people with whom children share their formative years to someone to count on when an extra egg is needed for that homemade bread. Opening heart and home to new friends who are coping with unpacking boxes, lining shelves, and finding their way around a new community is a wonderful way to show neighborly love.

Love You Can Touch for Adults

One thoughtful and sure-to-be appreciated idea for offering a helping hand while the new neighbors unload boxes is to bring them a large bag of chipped ice, plastic cups, and bottled water. The overwhelming task of locating their drinking glasses amidst the chaos will be solved with this quick pick-me-up. And after the practical is solved, the aesthetics can be addressed by cheering up their house that is currently full of bags and boxes.

A beautiful vase full of fragrant fresh flowers or a basket filled with scented candles and potpourri instantly creates a homelike atmosphere.

Love You Can Touch for Children

Decorate the outside of a clean pizza box with stickers and markers. Make a pretend pizza with construction paper and glue. Cut one piece of pizza out of the whole pie. Glue the pretend pizza into the box. Place a gift certificate for a pizza compliments of your family from the "best place" in the new neighborhood underneath the individual slice. Then place the individual slice on top of the certificate.

Love worth sharing can be taken to greater heights by your own personality and creations.

—SARAH CABANISS

7

Pasta Salad Served on Greens
Fresh Apricot Muffins
Chocolate Fudge Nut Cookies

*Recipes to Nourish
the Heart and Soul*

Pasta Salad Served on Greens
Serves: 6

Ingredients

    1 8-ounce package multicolored pasta, cooked according to package directions and drained
    1 cup cooked chicken breast shredded
    1 cup cooked turkey sausage, sliced
    1/2 cup corn
    1/4 cup green onion tops, sliced

Dressing

    1/2 cup bottled Italian salad dressing
    3 tablespoons mayonnaise
    1 tablespoon Dijon mustard
    1/2 teaspoon black pepper
    1 head Bibb lettuce, washed and separated

Directions

1. Place drained pasta in large glass mixing bowl.
2. Add remaining ingredients, except dressing.
3. In a small bowl stir together dressing ingredients.
4. Add dressing mixture to pasta and stir thoroughly. Chill.
5. Place lettuce on serving dish, then top with pasta mixture.

* Prepare an extra chicken breast and cut into small chunks. Place chicken chunks on toothpicks with an apricot mini muffin in between. Kids will love it!

Fresh Apricot Muffins
Makes: 1 dozen

Ingredients

    1 1/2 cups flour
    1/2 cup brown sugar
    2 teaspoons baking powder
    1/2 teaspoon salt
    1 teaspoon vanilla extract
    1 egg
    1/2 cup milk
    1/4 cup vegetable oil
    3/4 cup dried apricots, chopped

Directions

1. Combine dry ingredients in a medium mixing bowl.
2. Make a well in center of dry ingredients.
3. Add remaining ingredients, except apricots.
4. Stir just until moistened.
5. Fold apricots into muffin mixture.

6. Spoon batter into greased muffin tin, filling each about half way.
7. Bake at 400 degrees for 20 minutes or until golden brown.
8. Remove from pan immediately and cool on wire rack.

Chocolate Fudge Nut Cookies
Makes: 2 dozen

Ingredients
- 3 eggs, beaten
- 1 1/2 cups sugar
- 4 squares (4 ounces) unsweetened chocolate, melted
- 1/2 cup vegetable oil
- 2 teaspoons baking powder
- 2 teaspoons vanilla extract
- 1/2 teaspoon almond extract
- 2 cups flour
- 1/4 cup almonds, chopped
- cocoa powder (optional)

Directions
1. Combine all ingredients except flour and almonds in mixing bowl.
2. Slowly add flour and almonds to chocolate mixture, stirring until thoroughly combined.
3. Cover dough and chill for 1 hour.
4. Shape chilled dough into 1-inch balls and lightly dust with cocoa powder.
5. Place balls on ungreased cookie sheet. Bake at 375 degrees for 8 to 10 minutes.

* Leave the almonds out of part of the cookie dough—this can be the children's batch. Use white chocolate chips or small candy-coated chocolates to form smiley faces on the cookies.

Packaging Panache

Purchase cake boxes in graduated sizes from the local bakery. Place each menu item in a disposable container, then place them inside the cake boxes. Stack the boxes in order of size with the largest one on the bottom and tie them together with a wide, colorful ribbon.

A dinner of giggles and grins will keep the children entertained. Try making a simple dinner that includes smiling faces on each dinner item. An extra cake box covered with smiling faces will make a great container for your happy snacks. Try making sandwich smiles, wafer faces, and apple grins.

CHAPTER TWO

Just Because You're My Friend

I thank my God in all remembrance of you.
—THE BOOK OF PHILIPPIANS

A good friend is a gift from God's heart. In a true friendship both of you intimately know each other and like each other, "warts and all." A friend makes you feel special and you, in turn, want to make her feel special. The Golden Rule says: "Do for other people as you want them to do for you." Showing kindness and respect to a friend is easy because you hold them dear. It is always good for us to remind friends how important they are, especially when they are least expecting it. Express friendship by lending a helping hand in a particularly harried time, or do something special anytime just because you're friends.

Love You Can Touch for Adults

A stressed-out mom needs an extra pair of hands for assistance from time to time. She needs to feel loved, pampered, and appreciated, and you can be the one to make that happen! Give her a coupon for an afternoon (without children) in a favorite bookstore, preferably one that serves coffee and pastries. When she arrives home, have a simple and satisfying dinner ready to pop in the oven so her time away won't be so full of thinking of to-dos for when she returns. The gift of time is so precious.

Practice tenderhearted mercy and kindness to others…Most of all, let love guide your life.

—THE BOOK OF COLOSSIANS

Love You Can Touch for Children

An edible alphabet is cute, quick, and fun. A child loves to hear and see his or her name, and making it edible adds imagination as well as education. Purchase a prepared pound cake and slice pieces about 1 inch thick. Cut the child's name out of the slices, continuing until the name is spelled out. Sprinkle with colored powdered sugar and place in a tie box. (You can purchase the alphabet cookie cutters at craft stores.)

*Recipes to Nourish
the Heart and Soul*

Tortilla Club Sandwiches
Serves: 4

Ingredients
4 10-inch tortillas
1/2 cup refried beans
1 cup lettuce, shredded
1/4 cup sour cream
1 Tablespoon picante sauce
1 1/2 cups chicken, chopped
1/2 cup tomatoes, chopped
1/2 cup bacon, cooked and chopped
1/4 cup cheese, shredded

Directions
1. Place one tortilla on a large piece of wax paper. Spread entire surface of tortilla with refried beans. Sprinkle with lettuce.
2. Place another tortilla on top of the refried beans-and-lettuce layer. Cover with a damp paper towel while you combine sour cream and picante sauce. Next, spread a thin layer of sour cream dressing over top of tortilla. Sprinkle with chicken and tomatoes.
3. Place another tortilla over chicken and tomato mixture. Sprinkle with bacon and cheese. Top with remaining tortilla. Wrap with wax paper and place in refrigerator.

Sweet Potato Bundles
Serves: 4

Ingredients
2 large sweet potatoes, scrubbed
salt
black pepper
1 cup Canola oil
green onion tops (optional)

Directions
1. Peel and cut sweet potatoes lengthwise into strips 1/4- to 3/8-inch wide.
2. Toss sweet potatoes with salt and pepper.
3. Place oil in a skillet and heat on medium. Carefully place sweet potatoes in oil with spatula.
4. Fry for about 8 minutes, turning to cook evenly.
5. Remove and place on paper towels to drain.
6. Serve as is or tie in bundles with tops of green onions.

Alphabet Pound Cake
Makes: 1 10-inch pound cake

Ingredients
- 3 cups sugar
- 1 1/4 cups butter, softened
- 6 eggs
- 2 teaspoons vanilla extract
- 1/2 teaspoon almond extract
- 3 cups flour
- 1 teaspoon baking powder
- 1/4 teaspoon salt
- 1 cup whole milk

Directions
1. Grease and flour tube pan.
2. Preheat oven to 350 degrees.
3. Cream butter and sugar, add eggs one at a time.
4. Mix flour, baking powder, and salt in another bowl. Add to egg mixture alternately with milk on low speed.
5. Bake for 1 hour and 10 minutes or until a wooden toothpick in the center comes out clean.
6. Cool and remove from pan.
7. Cut 3/4-inch thick slices and lay out on wax paper.
8. Using alphabet cookie cutters, cut out letters to spell each name. Decorate with colored powdered sugar and sprinkles.

* If time does not allow for cake baking, purchase a frozen pound cake and complete steps 7 and 8.

Packaging Panache

A big basket full of interesting and delicious foods is always a welcome sight. Place the meal in a resealable plastic bag, then wrap in colored plastic wrap and place it in the basket. Add bright paper products, flavored waters, and tie boxes filled with the family members' names spelled out in pound cake letters for dessert.

CHAPTER 3

Children Going Off to School

Train up a child in the way he should go,
even when he is old he will not depart from it.
—THE BOOK OF PROVERBS

Milestones in a child's life are a constant reminder that a child stays in the home for a relatively short number of years. Watching a child grow and change every day is significant to how fast he or she really does grow up. The milestones are bittersweet. Everyone wants their child to grow, but sometimes it is hard to let go as they sprout their wings to fly. During these important life changes parents need some friendly support. Just a gentle reminder that they are doing their best to guide their child is priceless.

Love You Can Touch for Adults

If the child is going off to kindergarten, a colorful photo memory album that will record the highlights of each school year is a great gift for launching into this new phase of life. Place the memory book in a basket filled with freshly baked cookies, hot cocoa mix, and cute mugs. You can deliver it just after the child arrives home in the car or on the bus.

> *Children may close their ears to advice but they keep their eyes open to example.*
>
> —EDWINA PATTERSON

Love You Can Touch for Children

For the kindergarten kid, purchase a great monogrammed backpack and fill it with a Big Chief tablet, fat pencils, and a simple nonperishable snack.

If the young person is heading off to college, wrap a couple of tickets to the movies or a sporting event in a box of stationery that is filled with college stickers and stamps.

Nothing works better for college kids than a little box containing a prepaid phone card or some self-addressed, stamped envelopes, and stationery for letters home to the student's family. Keeping in touch helps new students hop the hurdle of homesickness. You might also want to include a set of his or her first healthful study snacks to help boost brain power.

Menu
Backpack Snack Dessert Mix
Peppermint Fudge
Power Popcorn

*Recipes to Nourish
the Heart and Soul*

Backpack Snack Dessert Mix
Makes: 6 cups

Ingredients
>   1 cup plain chocolate candies
>   1 cup chocolate-covered peanut candies
>   1 cup white chocolate morsels
>   1 cup gummy bears
>   1 cup malted milk balls
>   1 cup pretzel sticks

Directions

In a medium bowl combine all ingredients. Stir thoroughly until well mixed.

Peppermint Fudge
Makes: 2 dozen small pieces

Ingredients
>   1 1/2 cups sugar
>   2/3 cup evaporated milk

1/2 teaspoon salt
2 cups mini marshmallows
1 1/2 cups semi-sweet chocolate morsels
10 peppermint candies, crushed and divided
1/2 teaspoon peppermint extract
1 teaspoon vanilla extract
butter

Directions
1. In a medium saucepan mix sugar, milk, and salt over low heat.
2. Bring to a boil and simmer for four minutes.
3. Remove from heat and add marshmallows, chocolate morsels, peppermint candies, and extracts.
4. Pour into a buttered and greased 8 x 8 square pan and sprinkle the top with crushed peppermints.
5. Cover and place in refrigerator until firm.

Power Popcorn
Serves: 6-8

Ingredients
>   6 cups popped popcorn
>   3/4 cup sunflower seeds, shelled
>   3/4 cup currants

1/2 cup golden raisins
1/2 cup peanut butter
1 teaspoon butter

Directions
1. Place prepared popcorn in a large bowl.

2. Add sunflower seeds, currants, and raisins to popcorn.
3. Melt peanut butter and butter in a small saucepan over medium heat and pour over popcorn mixture.
4. Stir thoroughly to combine all ingredients.

Packaging Panache

For the kindergarten child, fill a brown paper bag with dessert mix. Tie the bag with a polka-dot ribbon and place in the monogrammed backpack.

For the college student, line some colorful Chinese food containers with tissue paper, then stuff with healthful study snacks.

Lunch and Munch More for Kids

Looking for something special for your child's lunch? Here are well-balanced, creative menus with a "Happy for the Heart" to tuck into a lunch box. Tasty foods will nourish the body and child-sized bits of inspiration will nourish the soul.

Noah's Ark Lunch
Pita boat filled with
    tuna salad
Animal cracker sandwiches—
    strawberry cream cheese
    with a slice of pear
Rainbow trail mix
Rain punch

Happy for the Heart: Plan a rainbow scavenger hunt to begin when your child arrives home from school. Leave his or her first clue on a red piece of paper in the lunchbox. Make up four other clues and write down each one on a different color of paper that represents the different colors of the rainbow. Scatter the clues throughout the house and yard, and have a special surprise waiting at the end of the rainbow.

Roly Poly Lunch
Tortilla and ham roll-up
Fruit roll-ups
Blueberries
Malted milk balls

Happy for the Heart: Place a golf ball in the lunchbox with a coupon for a trip to a putt-putt golf course the following weekend.

Stick-Up Lunch

Drumstick
Pretzel sticks
Celery sticks
Cheddar cheese sticks

Happy for the Heart: Play the "Pick a Person" game. Write on a notecard: "Pick a special someone who needs a happy thought, and after school together we will do something nice for that person."

The Kabob Job Lunch
Turkey chunks, cheese chunks, and mini-muffin kabob. Slide these items onto a blunt-ended kabob skewer, alternating as you go. This is a one-stop lunch on a stick.
Fruit kabob
Cake Kabob—Cube a slice of cake and slide onto a blunt-ended kabob skewer.

Happy for the Heart: Make a small coupon book using colorful sticky notes. Punch a hole in the top of the book and tie with a ribbon. Include coupons for a trip to the ice cream shop, a new small toy, a date with Mom for dinner, breakfast in bed, stay-up-late movie and popcorn night. Let the child redeem the coupons throughout the month.

Triangle Lunch

> Honey ham and sweet mustard sandwich
>   cut into triangle shapes
> Tortilla chips
> Cantaloupe triangles
> Brownie cut into triangle shapes

Happy for the Heart: Cut out a thin strip of paper and write "You're the Best" on it. Tuck the paper into a prepared fortune cookie. Place the cookie in a plastic bag and put it in the lunchbox.

New Zoo Review Lunch

> Elephant-shaped
>   peanut butter
>   sandwiches
> Monkey chow—dried bananas,
>   dried apricots,
>   golden raisins,
> honey-roasted
>   peanuts
> Animal crackers
> Jungle juice

Happy for the Heart: Trace an animal cookie cutter on some colored construction paper, cut it out, and write a note on it promising a trip to the zoo for both of you.

Leaves and Fishes Lunch

> Mini loaf of wheat bread,
>   split and filled with tuna salad
> Carrot fishing rods
> Fish-shaped pretzel crackers
> Gummy worms

Happy for the Heart: Place a package of fish stickers in the lunch box and include a note that says: "You're a great catch."

Muffin Madness Lunch

> Ham-and-cheese muffins
> BBQ baked potato chips
> Yogurt cup
> Dried cranberries

Happy for the Heart: Cut out the shape of an ice cream cone and another shape of a scoop of ice cream. Write on the ice cream scoop, "After school join me for an ice cream treat."

Chunk-a-Lunch

> Chicken chunks, ham chunks, or hot dog
>   chunks
> Vegetable chunks with dressing for
>   dipping
> Pineapple chunks
> Chocolate chunk cookies

Happy for the Heart: Place a small plastic toy in the lunchbox along with a poem that reads, "A trip to the toy store is what we'll do, to buy a new toy for you."

CHAPTER 4

Placing a Loved One in a Nursing Home

Gray hair is a crown of splendor...
—THE BOOK OF PROVERBS

*L*ife happens in seasons. As there is a season to be young, there is also a season to be old. It is very difficult for a family to make the decision to place a relative in a nursing home. It is a time when all sorts of emotions run through hearts as everyone tries to provide the best care available to this beloved person. This is a time when friends can offer needed support and assistance as both the family and the loved one in the nursing home adjust to a new way of life.

Love You Can Touch for Adults

Prepare a sampling of homemade frozen dinners, wrap with butcher paper, and affix labels on the outside of the containers for easy recognition. Include an inspirational book or favorite novel for reading as they reheat and eat their dinners. An emotionally and physically tired person will greatly enjoy this little act of love.

> *Freely we serve,*
> *because we freely love.*
> —John Milton

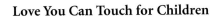

Love You Can Touch for Children

Prepare a "You're the Best" calendar for the child. Include stickers, stamps, and cutout hearts. In a note to the child's parents, explain that this calendar can help the child track his or her "sharing of sunshine" with the loved one in the nursing home. Make a plan for small "happys" that the child can do to show the grandparent or other relative he or she is still thought about, loved, and considered a vital part of the family. Encourage the child to send pictures of happy times together, special art projects, yummy cookies, and some stamped, self-addressed envelopes to be sent back to the child.

If the nursing home allows, take a gentle pet and children in for a visit.

*Recipes to Nourish
the Heart and Soul*

Shrimp, Cheese, and Cilantro Manicotti
Serves: 4

Ingredients
> 8 manicotti shells
> 1 10-3/4 ounce can cream of celery soup
> 1/2 cup sour cream
> 2 cups cooked shrimp, chopped
> 1 4-ounce can green chilies
> 2 Tablespoons cilantro, finely chopped
> 1/2 cup yellow onion, finely chopped
> 2 Tablespoons butter
> 1/2 cup pepperjack cheese, shredded

Directions
1. Prepare manicotti shells according to package directions, drain, and set aside.
2. Combine soup and sour cream; stir well.
3. Combine shrimp, green chilies, cilantro, and half of soup and sour cream mixture.
4. Stuff manicotti shells with shrimp mixture. Place in a baking dish.
5. Sauté onion and butter in a medium skillet until tender. Stir reserved soup mixture in with sautéed onions and spoon over manicotti.
6. Bake uncovered for 15 minutes. Remove, sprinkle with cheese, and bake again until melted.

Colorful Confetti Corn Salad
Serves: 4

Ingredients
> 1 12-ounce package frozen corn, defrosted
> 3 green onion tops, chopped
> 1 small red pepper, finely chopped
> 1 Tablespoon fresh parsley, chopped

2 Tablespoons red wine vinegar
1 Tablespoon Canola oil
salt and pepper to taste

Directions
1. In a medium bowl combine all ingredients. Cover and chill overnight.

Bread Batons
Makes: 6 Batons

Ingredients
1/4 cup butter, softened
1 cup Cheddar cheese, grated
1/2 cup sour cream
1 cup flour
1/2 teaspoon garlic, chopped

Directions
1. Cream butter and add cheese and sour cream. Mix thoroughly to combine.
2. Combine flour and garlic. Slowly add to creamed mixture, blending until smooth.
3. Place dough on a lightly floured work surface. Divide dough in half and roll it to a 12 x 7 rectangle. Cut into 1/2-inch strips. Repeat with other dough.
4. Twist dough strips two or three times or make into heart shapes and place on a greased cookie sheet.
5. Bake at 350 degrees for 10 to 12 minutes.

Packaging Panache

Place homemade frozen dinners in colorful freezer-safe containers, wrap with butcher paper, and affix decorative labels including recipe name and the date prepared on the outside of the containers for easy freezer recognition.

CHAPTER 5

Weddings

And the greatest of these is love.
—THE BOOK OF 1 CORINTHIANS

A wedding day is full of anticipation and dreams of future hopes and promises. Days do not get much more special than the day on which two people in love are married. Friends and family gather to wish the happy couple the best as they enter into a new phase of life blooming with hopeful happiness. Meaningful gifts with a touch of sentiment make this moment even more special. Friend or loved ones can recall what meant the most to them and pass on a gift of love and caring to the new couple.

As most wedding celebrations focus on the elegant and fancy, a gift of fresh pizza and delicious ice cream sandwiches will really hit the spot.

Love You Can Touch for Adults

Purchase three matching frames. Have pictures of the bride's and groom's parents on their wedding day long ago matted and framed. Present your gift to the newlyweds along with a promise to frame their favorite wedding photo to match.

Love You Can Touch for Children

If this happens to be a second marriage for either the bride or groom, children could be involved. Varying emotions and uncertainty might be the order of the day as the children watch their father or mother marry another person. You can help reassure the children that they are loved, appreciated, and cherished by the new family as well as by their original family. The heart-shaped ice cream sandwiches are a perfect addition to a special children's gift box. The gift box could include, children's books about blended families, stamped envelopes for letters to the child's other parent, and some personalized stationery.

In dreams and love there are no impossibilities.

—JANOS ARANY

25

Menu
Heart-Shaped Pizza
Spinach Apple Salad
Heart-Shaped Ice Cream Sandwiches

*Recipes to Nourish
the Heart and Soul*

Heart-Shaped Pizza
Serves: 4

Ingredients
>   1 large prepared pizza crust
>   1 jar spaghetti or pizza sauce
>   1/2 pound ground round, cooked and
>   drained
>   1/2 cup green pepper, diced
>   1/4 cup yellow onion, diced and lightly
>   sautéed
>   1/4 cup bacon, cooked and chopped
>   1 cup mozzarella, shredded
>   1/2 cup Parmesan, shredded
>   black olives, chopped (optional)

Directions
1. With kitchen shears, cut a large heart shape out of the round pizza crust.
2. Spread a thick layer of spaghetti or pizza sauce over top of crust.
3. Layer with other ingredients, in order of listing.
4. Bake at 375 degrees for 15 minutes or until warmed through.

* Some pizza places will sell or give you an empty pizza box. Cover it with contact paper and decorate in a wedding motif.

Spinach Apple Salad
Serves: 4

Ingredients
>   2 cups fresh spinach, washed and torn
>   1 large apple, cored and cut into small
>   pieces
>   3/4 cup sliced fresh mushrooms

Dressing
>   2 Tablespoons Canola oil
>   1 Tablespoon lemon juice
>   1 Tablespoon honey
>   1/2 teaspoon garlic, chopped
>   1/4 cup sliced almonds, toasted

Directions
1. Place spinach in large salad bowl. Add apples and mushrooms. Toss lightly to mix.
2. In a screwtop jar combine dressing ingredients. Cover and shake well. When ready to serve, pour dressing over salad. Toss lightly to coat and sprinkle with toasted almonds.

* To keep apples from browning, brush with a lemon juice-and-water mixture. The water will reduce the lemon flavor on the apples and the juice will keep the apples from turning brown.

Heart-Shaped Ice Cream Sandwiches
Makes: 6 sandwiches

Ingredients
1 box chocolate fudge cake mix
1 half-gallon premium ice cream, like
    chocolate swirl, raspberry cream, or
    peppermint
fresh raspberries
1 pint whipping cream, whipped
1 teaspoon vanilla

Directions
1. Line bottom of jelly roll pan with wax or parchment paper. Spray a light coat of cooking spray.
2. Prepare cake according to package directions. Package directions will probably *not* call for using a jelly roll pan. Reduce baking time because of a larger pan and thus a thinner spreading of batter.
3. Soften ice cream and spread in bottom of jelly roll pan. If you like, stir fresh raspberries into softened ice cream. Place in freezer to refreeze.
4. When cake has baked and cooled, pick up sides of wax paper or parchment and lift it out of pan. Using your large heart cookie cutter, cut heart shapes from cooked cake, then set aside.
5. Once ice cream has frozen, cut hearts from ice cream too. Place heart-shaped ice cream in between two heart-shaped cakes. Wrap tightly in wax or parchment paper and place in freezer. Repeat process until you are out of cake hearts. Once all ice cream sandwiches have been prepared, place them in a resealable freezer bag and freeze until firm.
6. Whip cream and vanilla and place in a small container.

Packaging Panache

Put the pizza in a decorated pizza box and adorn the wax or parchment paper covering the heart-shaped ice cream sandwiches with wedding stickers. Fill the bottom of a heart-shaped box with lots of plastic wrap and place the salad inside, putting the dressing in a separate container with a lid. (If you have extra stickers, place them on the outside of the container.) Put the entire meal in a large storage container and wrap the lid with an extension cord "bow"— two items every couple will need!

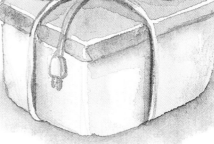

CHAPTER 6

New Baby

Like arrows in the hands of a warrior are sons born in one's youth.
Blessed is the man whose quiver is full of them.

—THE BOOK OF PSALMS

B·A·B·Y

The greatest gift of all comes in the smallest package.

No one can explain the wondrous range of emotions parents feel when they have a brand-new baby. They marvel that no one has had a child just like theirs. And a new baby is truly an occasion for witnessing a miracle—the miracle of life and birth. A little child is the parents' to protect, teach, and prepare for a life of goodness and joy. The Book of Proverbs says, "Train up a child in the way that he should go and when he is old he will not depart from it." As the new parents begin the wonderful task of raising their new little member of the family, friends can step in to provide much-needed help and support. These gift ideas offer you a golden opportunity to make the first few weeks or months a little easier for them.

Love You Can Touch for Adults

Purchase a tree from a local nursery and have it planted in the yard of the newborn's home. Create a certificate dedicating the tree to the child. Have your picture taken with the child in front of the tree.

Love You Can Touch for Children

When you visit a new baby, it is important that you first greet the older child or children. Ask the older child to introduce you to "his" or "her" new baby.

When bringing your gift for the newborn, be sure to include a little something for the older child.

Books on becoming a new big brother or big sister are a helpful way to ease the stress of a new little person in the home. The older sibling needs to feel just as important as he or she did before the birth of the new family member. Bring a bunch of colorful balloons or a birthday cake for the sibling to celebrate his or her day of becoming a big brother or a big sister.

Every child born into the world is a new thought of God, an ever-fresh and radiant possibility.

—KATE DOUGLAS WIGGIN

Menu
Berry Bread
Ham and Pineapple Bread with
Brown Sugar Butter
Tin of Flavored Teas

*Recipes to Nourish
the Heart and Soul*

Berry Bread
Makes: 1 loaf

Ingredients
> 1 1/2 cups flour
> 3/4 teaspoon ginger
> 1/2 teaspoon baking soda
> 1/4 teaspoon nutmeg
> 1/4 teaspoon salt
> 2 eggs, beaten
> 1 cup sugar
> 3/4 cup raspberries, mashed
> 1/2 cup blueberries, mashed
> 1/4 cup cooking oil
> 1 1/2 teaspoons lemon rind,
>   finely shredded

> 1 cup sliced almonds, optional

Directions
1. In a medium bowl combine flour, ginger, baking soda, nutmeg, and salt.
2. In another bowl combine eggs, sugar, mashed berries, oil, and lemon peel.
3. Add to flour mixture, stirring just until combined. Fold in nuts.
4. Place in a greased 9 x 5 x 3-inch loaf pan. Bake at 350 degrees for 1 hour or until a toothpick inserted in center comes out clean. Remove from pan and cool on a wire rack.

Ham and Pineapple Bread
Makes : 1 loaf

Ingredients
> 1 cup flour
> 1 teaspoon cinnamon
> 1 teaspoon baking soda
> 1/4 teaspoon salt
> 1/4 teaspoon baking powder
> 1/4 teaspoon ground nutmeg
> 2/3 cup sugar
> 1 8 1/4-ounce can crushed pineapple,
>   drained (reserve 2 Tablespoons of
>   juice)
> 1 cup ham, diced
> 1/4 cup cooking oil
> 1 egg

Directions

1. In a mixing bowl combine flour, cinnamon, baking soda, salt, baking powder, and nutmeg.
2. In another bowl combine sugar, crushed pineapple and reserved juice, ham, cooking oil, and egg. Mix well.
3. Add flour mixture and stir just until combined. Pour batter into a greased 8 x 4 x 2-inch loaf pan.
4. Bake at 350 degrees for 50 minutes or until a toothpick inserted in center comes out clean. Cool.
5. Remove bread from loaf pan and cool on a wire rack.

Brown Sugar Butter
Makes: 3/4 cup

Ingredients

1 3-ounce package cream cheese, softened
1/4 cup butter, softened

Packaging Panache

Fill a diaper holder with a variety of breads wrapped in colored plastic wrap, accompanying spreads, and freezer instructions. This will give the new parents something quick to serve to guests who come over to visit the new baby.

1/4 cup brown sugar
1 teaspoon vanilla extract

Directions

Combine ingredients in a food processor bowl and process until smooth. Transfer to a storage container and refrigerate until chilled.

* To make maple butter, replace brown sugar with 1/4 cup powdered sugar and vanilla extract with 1 teaspoon maple extract.

15 Ways to Wrap Your Gifts Without Wrapping Paper

Hatboxes—Fill a hatbox with tissue paper, shredded colored paper, or colored cellophane. Place your gift in the center and fill in the empty spaces with your desired stuffing.

Wooden Cheese Boxes—These wooden boxes are perfect for stenciling, painting, monogramming, or for gluing on buttons and bows. Try stuffing the insides with a yard of velvet, flannel, or netting, whichever best matches the theme chosen for the outside of your box.

Mailing Tubes—You can find mailing tubes in all different colors. Select your favorite and decorate with stamps, stickers, and small ribbons. Fill the inside of the tube with confetti, dried beans, small pine cones, shredded paper, or fabric. Place your gift inside and seal with the lid. (You might want to issue a word of warning before the confetti flies everywhere!)

Splatter-Painted Wooden Crates—You can find these wooden crates at a farmer's market or at your local grocery store. First dust the crates off with a towel. Purchase some craft paints with a squirtable top, place the crate on some newspaper, and splatter with paint. (Kids love this!) Let dry thoroughly, then line with fabric or raffia.

Aluminum Foil—Pull out several long sheets of foil, place your gift in the center, pull the foil up and around the gift, and twist just like a chocolate kiss. Tuck a note in the top on some white paper so it resembles the top of a chocolate kiss. This is great gift wrap for a chocolate lover!

Glass Carafes—Fill a glass carafe halfway with little pebbles, small shells, pennies, or corn kernels. Place a small gift in the middle and fill the rest with pebbles, shells, fresh cranberries, or whatever filler you choose until the gift is covered. Place a small handkerchief on the top of the carafe and secure it with a rubber band and a colorful ribbon. This will be like finding a prize in a Cracker Jack box.

Galvanized Buckets—Fill the inside of the bucket with raffia, shredded paper, crumpled tissue paper, or various colors of yarn. Tie a large plaid bow around the perimeter of the bucket.

Chinese Take-Out Containers—Line the inside of a Chinese take-out container with cellophane or tissue. Place your gift inside, close the container, and tie the top with a large ribbon.

Burlap Bags—Line the inside of the bag with cotton or fabric. Tie the bag with raffia or a plaid ribbon.

Canning Jars—Remove several labels from cans in your pantry. Place them facing outward around the perimeter of the glass canning jar so that the gift will remain a mystery until opened. Set the gift inside the jar and top with the lid. Put a small piece of fabric on the lid and screw the top over the fabric.

Hollowed-Out Pumpkin—Line a hollowed-out pumpkin with green florist paper or plastic wrap. Fill individual plastic bags with the dry ingredients for pumpkin-cranberry bread. Top the pumpkin with its lid and tie the recipe to the stem.

Clear Acrylic Boxes—Line the box with florist paper, tissue, or newspaper. Top with a lid and place a large ribbon under the bottom of the box, tying a bow at the top. (Fabric ribbon that has a wire on both edges makes the best bow.)

Colored Netting—Fabric stores have great wrapping paper alternatives! Buy about a yard of netting, depending on the size of the gift. Place the gift inside and pull the netting up over the gift. Secure with a rubber band and tie with a long piece of ric-rac.

Mixing Bowl and Food Section—Fill the mixing bowl with ingredients of a favorite recipe. Cover the top of the bowl with the food section from your newspaper and secure with kitchen twine or raffia.

Little Themed Boxes—Many stores sell gingerbread man-shaped boxes, star-shaped boxes, heart-shaped boxes, and bunny-shaped boxes. Fill the inside of a themed box with cookies to match the theme. Little gingerbread men placed in baking papers and then in the matching box will make a perfect "Thinking of You" gift, no matter what the season or occasion.

CHAPTER 7
Moving

Dear friend, I pray that you may enjoy good health
and that all may go well with you...
—THE BOOK OF 3 JOHN

It is always a sad day when friends or family members move to a new city, new state, or even a new country. However, new job opportunities and other life changes cause many people to relocate and start their lives over in a brand new place. And moving is such an overwhelming process—all of the good-byes, the change of address cards, the hassle of setting up home all over again.

Try to get together several reliable people who can come and help load boxes for the movers. This would also be a great time to pick up some finger foods from the grocery store and take some time out for a little packing party.

Love You Can Touch for Adults

Send a humorous card to your friends' new address so it is waiting for them when they arrive. Tuck in a phone card worth so many free minutes or hours so they can call and keep you updated on their settling-in progress. Let them know that you will be thinking and praying for them as they adjust to their new home and neighborhood.

> We are shaped and fashioned by what we love.
>
> —GOETHE

Love You Can Touch for Children

Send separate cards to the family's children. Include some of their favorite things in the envelope. Try shipping a little package just after they have arrived as a reminder that someone far away is thinking of them.

Menu
Full Meal Deal Muffins
Fruited Granola
Confetti Brownies
Fresh Fruits

Recipes to Nourish the Heart and Soul

Full Meal Deal Muffins
Serves: 12

Ingredients
- 1 cup all-purpose flour
- 1/2 cup whole wheat flour
- 2 teaspoons baking powder
- 1/4 teaspoon salt
- 1 egg, beaten
- 3/4 cup milk
- 1/4 cup honey
- 1/4 cup vegetable oil
- 1/2 cup ham, chopped
- 1/4 cup cheddar cheese, shredded
- 1/8 cup green onion tops, chopped

Directions
1. In a mixing bowl stir together flour, whole wheat flour, baking powder,

and salt. Make a well in center of dry ingredients.
2. In a small mixing bowl combine egg, milk, honey, and oil. Add to dry ingredients, stirring just until moistened.
3. Fold in ham, cheese, and green onions.
4. Line muffin tin with baking cups and fill two-thirds full.
5. Bake at 400 degrees for 20 minutes or until golden brown.

Fruited Granola
Makes: 3 cups

Ingredients
   1 1/2 cups rolled oats
   1/2 cup coconut
   1/2 cup sliced almonds
   1/2 cup sunflower seeds
   1/2 cup honey
   1/3 cup Canola oil
   1/4 teaspoon ginger
   1/2 cup dried peaches
   1/2 cup dried cranberries

Directions
   1. In a bowl stir together rolled oats, coconut, almonds, and sunflower seeds.
   2. In another bowl stir together honey, oil, and ginger; stir into oat mixture.
   3. Fold in peaches and cranberries.

4. Spread mixture evenly in greased jelly roll pan.
5. Bake at 300 degrees for 30 to 35 minutes or until browned.
6. Cool and break into clumps. Store in tightly covered jars or plastic bags.

Confetti Brownies
Serves: 12

Ingredients
   2 squares unsweetened chocolate
   2/3 cup shortening
   2 cups sugar
   4 eggs, lightly beaten
   2 teaspoons vanilla extract
   1 1/2 cups flour
   1 teaspoon baking powder
   1 teaspoon salt

Directions
   1. Preheat oven to 350 degrees.
   2. In a saucepan heat chocolate and shortening over low heat, stirring constantly until melted.
   3. Remove from heat and stir in sugar, eggs, and vanilla extract.
   4. Stir in remaining ingredients and pour into a greased 13 x 9 x 2-inch baking dish. Bake for 25 minutes or until wooden toothpick inserted in middle comes out clean.

Chocolate Icing

Ingredients
> 2 cups milk chocolate morsels
> 4 Tablespoons cream
> 2 teaspoons vanilla extract

Directions
> 1. Place ingredients in a microwave-safe bowl and microwave on medium power for 40 second intervals, stirring between intervals until melted.
> 2. Pour icing over prepared brownies.
> 3. Sprinkle liberally with your favorite choice of confetti (chocolate candies, gumdrops, sprinkles, gummy bears, jelly beans, etc.).

Fresh Fruits

Ingredients
> selection of fresh fruits
> store-bought dips

Directions
> Use resealable plastic bags to transport your fruits and dips.

Packaging Panache

Pack a box full of your friends' favorite snacks, including some fresh-baked muffins and ground coffee that can be the first breakfast in their new home. Wrap the box in a map from their new city and tie with raffia. You may want to include funny little notes throughout the box to lighten spirits during the tiring task of unpacking.

CHAPTER 8
Illness in Family

May your unfailing love be my comfort.
—The Book of Psalms

An illness in a family is a constant concern and an emotional drain on everyone. It truly is a time for consistent caring and support to be shown to each of the family members. Going in for tests, waiting for results, and dealing with pain is a process that is incredibly trying. When one member of a family is experiencing an illness, it is a good time for friends to show their love and support for everyone who is dealing with the trauma. Just offering a chauffeur service for errands or a little "Thinking of You" bouquet of flowers can make a big difference.

Love You Can Touch for Adults

Make a little coupon book for the family member who is the main caretaker of the sick person. Include ideas such as running errands for a day, picking up the children after school, organizing a group of neighbors to bring over dinner several times a week, or setting up a sitter service to help care for the ill person. A simple gesture like keeping the cookie jar full or taking the caregiver out for coffee can help lift spirits. Tie a brightly colored ribbon around the coupon book and put a note on the top that explains how and when the recipient can redeem his or her coupons.

> *Love cures people—both the ones who give it and the ones who receive it.*
>
> —KARL MENNINGER

Love You Can Touch for Children

A bundle of books and a sack of snacks make a great pair. Gather up a selection of books that are of interest to children. Place these items in a big plastic tote with a lid. The child can even turn the tote upside down and use it for a desk! This works particularly well if little ones have to wait in a hospital room for long periods of time.

Menu
Lentil Vegetable Soup
Cornbread with Cheese
Five-Fruit Crisp Cookies

Recipes to Nourish the Heart and Soul

Lentil Vegetable Soup
Serves: 6-8

Ingredients

1 1/2 cups dried lentils
1 cup yellow onion or leeks, chopped
2 cloves garlic, chopped
1 Tablespoon vegetable oil
5 cups chicken broth
1 16-ounce can diced tomatoes
1 Tablespoon Worcestershire sauce
1 cup carrots, chopped
4 medium potatoes, peeled and cubed
1/2 cup celery, chopped
1/2 teaspoon salt
1/4 teaspoon pepper
1 cup chicken, chopped
chopped parsley (optional)

Directions

1. Rinse lentils and set aside. In a large saucepan sauté onion and garlic until lightly browned.
2. Add chicken broth, tomatoes, and Worcestershire. Bring to a boil, reduce heat, cover and simmer for 15 minutes.
3. Add remaining ingredients, bring to a boil again, reduce heat, cover and simmer for 30 additional minutes.

Cornbread with Cheese
Makes: 6 muffins

Ingredients

1 box cornbread mix, prepared according to package directions
1/4 cup Cheddar cheese, shredded
1 teaspoon sugar

Directions

1. In a medium mixing bowl prepare cornbread mix according to package directions. Stir in cheese and sugar.
2. Spray muffin pan with cooking spray and fill muffin cups two-thirds full.
3. Bake according to package directions on cornbread.

Five-Fruit Crisp Cookies
Makes: 2 dozen

Ingredients

3/4 cup butter
1 3/4 cup flour
1 1/4 cups brown sugar
1 egg
1 teaspoon baking powder
2 teaspoons vanilla

1/4 teaspoon baking soda
2 cups rolled oats

Five-Fruit Filling
    1 3/4 cups fruit, peeled and chopped
      (pears, dried cranberries, dried
      cherries, apricots, apples)
    1/2 cup sugar
    2 Tablespoons fruit juice

Directions
1. Cream butter in a medium mixing bowl. Combine with half of flour.
2. Add remaining ingredients, except rolled oats. Stir to combine.
3. Add oats and mix thoroughly. Spoon onto ungreased cookie sheet.
4. Using back of spoon, make an indention in the middle of each cookie. Set aside.

Fruit Filling
1. Combine fruits, sugar, and fruit juice in a small saucepan. Bring to a boil, stirring constantly until liquid evaporates.
2. Place one teaspoon of fruit filling into indentations in each unbaked cookie.
3. Bake at 350 degrees for 10 to 12 minutes.

Packaging Panache

Purchase a large, colorful ceramic pot and place a big, resealable plastic bag inside that is filled with the soup. Wrap the cornbread in a dinner-sized cloth napkin, tie the napkin at the top, and place it on top of the sealed plastic bag. Repeat with cookies. Everything will stay warm this way. The recipient can use the pot for a plant. (You may even want to bring one on your next visit.)

5 Great Meals to Freeze

No one ever plans an accident or an emergency, or even a baby's early delivery. Having a simple repertoire of easy-to-prepare, freezable items will make spontaneous gift giving of foods a simple way to share love and support. Try preparing these recipes ahead of time and freezing them for future use.

Freezer Teasers

Frozen foods keep best when they are wrapped and stored properly. Here are some helpful suggestions for freezer storage:

- *Cool Foods First:* Let foods come to room temperature before freezing. This way the dish will freeze faster and won't raise the temperature of your freezer.

- *No Guessing Here:* Before freezing, label each package with the name of the dish, the date prepared, and defrosting and cooking instructions. This information is handy just in case the recipe gets lost. If you are using aluminum foil, you can write directly on the foil with a permanent marking pen.

- *Think Before You Thaw:* Thaw frozen foods still foil-wrapped in the refrigerator on a tray. Some dishes can be defrosted in the microwave; remember to remove the foil first. Thawing foods at room temperature may promote spoilage and bacteria growth.

Three-Cheese Baked Potatoes
Serves: 4

Ingredients
    4 medium baking potatoes
    vegetable oil
    1/2 cup sour cream

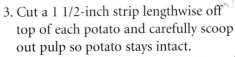

1/4 cup milk or half-and-half
1/4 cup butter
1/8 cup Cheddar cheese, shredded
1/8 cup Parmesan cheese, shredded
1/8 cup blue cheese, crumbled (substitute
    Edam cheese if preferred)
1/2 teaspoon salt
1/4 teaspoon pepper
cooked and crumbled bacon, 1/4 cup
    chopped chives (optional)

Directions
1. Wash potatoes and rub skins with oil. Bake at 400 degrees for one hour.
2. Remove from oven and let cool thoroughly.

3. Cut a 1 1/2-inch strip lengthwise off top of each potato and carefully scoop out pulp so potato stays intact.
4. In a medium mixing bowl combine potato pulp and remaining ingredients.
5. Beat with a mixer until light and fluffy; fill shells with mixture.

To freeze: Wrap each potato in aluminum foil. Place in a resealable plastic freezer bag and place in freezer.

To reheat: When ready to cook, remove from freezer and defrost 20 minutes. Preheat oven to 400 degrees. Place foil-wrapped potatoes on cookie sheet. Bake for 20 minutes in oven or until warmed.

Sweet-and-Sour Meatloaf with Chive Polenta
Serves: 6-8

Ingredients
3 slices wheat bread
1/2 cup medium yellow onion, peeled and roughly chopped
2 cloves garlic, peeled and chopped
1/2 cup ketchup
2 teaspoons dry mustard
1 1/2 pounds ground round
2 large eggs, beaten
2 teaspoons salt

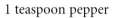

1 teaspoon pepper
1 teaspoon Tabasco
Sauce
　3 Tablespoons ketchup
　2 Tablespoons brown sugar
　2 1/2 teaspoons dried mustard

Directions
1. Preheat oven to 400 degrees. Remove crust from bread.
2. Process bread crumbs in a food processor until fine. Place bread crumbs in a large mixing bowl.
3. Add onion to food processor and process until fine. Add to bread crumbs.
4. Add garlic, ketchup, mustard, ground round, eggs, and seasonings to mixing bowl. Knead together with hands until thoroughly mixed.
5. Using your hands, form an elongated loaf. Place meatloaf on a wire rack and then on a jelly roll pan (cookie sheet with sides).
6. In a small bowl combine the sauce ingredients. Stir thoroughly to combine. Using a pastry brush, brush top of meatloaf with sauce.
7. Bake for about 35 minutes or until a meat thermometer registers 160 degrees.

To freeze: Cool completely, wrap tightly with aluminum foil, and place in freezer in a resealable freezer bag.

To reheat: Defrost for about 30 minutes. Preheat oven to 400 degrees. Place on a cookie sheet and cover with foil. Place in oven for 20 minutes or until heated.

Chive Polenta
Serves: 4 - 6

Ingredients
　2 cups water
　1 1/2 teaspoons salt
　1 cup corn kernels
　1/2 cup fresh chives, chopped
　2 cups quick-cooking polenta
　4 Tablespoons butter
　1/2 teaspoon pepper

Directions
1. In a medium saucepan combine 2 cups of water, salt, corn, and milk.
2. Place on high heat and bring to a boil. Slowly pour polenta into saucepan, stirring constantly.
3. Reduce heat to low. Simmer, stirring often, until polenta is thick, about 6 minutes.
4. Stir in chives, butter, and pepper.

To freeze: Cool and place in resealable freezer bag. Label with recipe name and date.

To reheat: Defrost for 30 minutes, add to a medium saucepan with a little water and milk. Stir until thoroughly heated.

Fresh Tomato Corn and Pasta Pie
Serves: 6

Ingredients
- 1/2 12-ounce package spaghetti
- 2 Tablespoons butter
- 1/3 cup Parmesan cheese, grated
- 2 eggs
- 2 cups tomatoes, chopped
- 1 cup corn
- 1/2 cup carrot, shredded
- 1/3 cup onion, chopped
- 3/4 teaspoon dried oregano
- 1 clove garlic, finely chopped

Directions
1. Cook pasta according to package directions, drain.
2. Stir butter and Parmesan cheese into hot pasta, cool.
3. Add eggs to mixture and stir well.
4. Place pasta mixture in 10-inch pie plate. Use back of spoon to shape pasta into a pie shell. Bake at 350 degrees for 8 minutes or until set.
5. In a medium bowl combine remaining ingredients. Pour into pasta pie shell and bake for 20 minutes.

To freeze: Wrap pie tightly with aluminum foil.

Place in a resealable freezer bag. Write date on a piece of masking tape and place on freezer bag.

To reheat: When ready to bake, preheat oven to 350 degrees and bake for 30 minutes or until warmed.

Herb Dumpling and Chicken Casserole
Serves: 6

Ingredients

2 cups self-rising flour
2 Tablespoons fresh or dried herbs, chopped
3/4 cup milk
1/4 cup oil
6 boneless, skinless chicken breasts
4 cups water, chicken stock, or chicken broth
3 chicken bouillon cubes
1/2 teaspoon salt
1/4 teaspoon pepper
1 small yellow onion, quartered
2 stalks celery, broken into pieces
any extra fresh herbs that you like

Directions

1. Place water, chicken stock, or chicken broth in a large stock pot.
2. Add bouillon cubes, seasonings, onion, celery, and herbs. Add chicken and boil until cooked. Remove chicken and place in large casserole dish.
3. Mix together flour, herbs, milk, and oil and roll out onto floured surface. Cut into 1 1/2-inch strips and cut strips into 2-inch pieces. Add dumplings to boiling chicken broth. Do not stir. Cook for 20 minutes on medium heat. Remove dumplings and place on top of chicken.
4. Add 1 cup milk and 1 stick butter. Cook until butter is melted.
5. Pour sauce over the chicken and dumplings and let cool.

To freeze: Cover very tightly with plastic wrap and then aluminum foil. Label and place into a jumbo freezer bag and into freezer.

To reheat: Defrost for about 30 minutes. Preheat oven to 400 degrees. Remove plastic wrap and cover with foil. Bake for 20 minutes or until warmed.

Peanut Butter Cake with Peanut Butter Cup Ice Cream
Serves: 12

Ingredients

3/4 cup butter, softened
1 cup creamy peanut butter
2 cups firmly packed brown sugar

3 eggs
2 cups all-purpose flour
1 Tablespoon baking powder
1/2 teaspoon salt
1 cup milk
2 teaspoons vanilla

Directions
1. In a medium saucepan cream together butter and peanut butter. Gradually add sugar, beating well at medium speed with an electric mixer.
2. Add eggs one at a time, beating well after each addition.
3. Combine flour, baking powder, and salt. Add dry ingredients alternately with milk to creamed mixture, beginning and ending with flour mixture. Mix after each addition. Stir in vanilla.
4. Pour batter into a greased and floured 13 x 9 x 2-inch pan. Bake for 40 to 45 minutes.

To freeze: Wrap tightly with plastic wrap and then with foil. Label and place in a jumbo freezer bag, then into freezer.

Peanut Butter Cup Ice Cream
Makes: 1 quart

Ingredients
1 quart vanilla bean ice cream
1 cup peanut butter cups, roughly chopped

Directions
1. Place ice cream in a food processor and process until smooth.
2. Add peanut butter cups and process until combined.
3. Place ice cream in a plastic container with lid. Put back in freezer to freeze until firm.

CHAPTER 9
Death in Family

Blessed are those who mourn, for they will be comforted.
—The Book of Matthew

*I*t is difficult for people to understand the pain of losing a loved one unless they, too, have experienced it. One minute the person is here and the next minute he or she is gone. Those who are left must deal with the roller coaster of grief and emotion that no one can explain. And most people feel unsure of how to treat a friend who has lost someone special. Telling a friend, "I know exactly how you feel," is actually not the best thing to say. It's better to admit, "I don't know how you feel." Providing true solace requires a willingness to stand by the person in pain, no matter how long and difficult the mourning period may seem. The comforter's role is not to orchestrate the healing process but to keep the friend company through difficulties. In other words, it's important to just be there.

If you'd like to provide food in this situation, think ahead to future nights where cooking will not be a priority, and plan to make foods that will freeze well. I recommend tripling the Chicken, Spinach, and Artichoke Lasagna and Cherry

Chess Tart recipes. You can give two portions to your friend (mark the one for the freezer with the date and baking directions) and keep one for your family to allow you more time to help out.

Love You Can Touch for Adults

Purchase some beautiful writing paper in a soft color and write a note to the family telling them how much their loved one meant to you. Include a personal recollection and don't worry if it also happens to be humorous. Family members will enjoy remembering pleasant times. You also might want to send an underprivileged child to a special camp in honor of the person who passed away.

> *We can comfort those in any trouble with the comfort we ourselves have received from God.*
>
> —The Book of 2 Corinthians

Love You Can Touch for Children

Assemble a "You Are Special" box for the family's children. Include fruits, candies, chips, and other favorite treats, plus an "I Love You" note to each child. Place a little note in his or her pocket, and tuck in a dollar bill to buy a candy bar, soda, or hot chocolate.

Menu

Chicken, Spinach, and Artichoke Lasagna
Golden Raisin Wheat Loaf
Cherry Chess Tart

*Recipes to Nourish
the Heart and Soul*

Chicken, Spinach,
and Artichoke Lasagna
Serves: 8

Ingredients

2 cups chicken breast, cooked and cubed
1 clove garlic, chopped
1 16-ounce can tomatoes, undrained
2 6-ounce cans tomato paste
2 eggs
1 16-ounce carton ricotta cheese
1 10-ounce package frozen chopped
    spinach, thawed and drained
1 small can artichoke hearts, drained
    and chopped
1 8-ounce package lasagna noodles,
    cooked according to package directions
1/2 cup Parmesan cheese, grated
1 6-ounce package mozzarella cheese slices

Directions

1. In a medium saucepan combine chicken, garlic, tomatoes, and tomato paste. Heat thoroughly, stirring to combine.

2. In a medium bowl combine eggs, ricotta, spinach, and artichokes.

3. Spread about 1/2 cup chicken and tomato sauce into baking dish.

4. Layer half of the cooked lasagna noodles, ricotta mixture, mozzarella cheese slices, then chicken/tomato sauce. Repeat layers.

5. Top with Parmesan cheese and cover and bake at 350 degrees for 30 minutes.

Golden Raisin Wheat Loaf
Makes: 1 loaf

Ingredients

1 package dry yeast
1 cup warm milk (105 degrees)
1/2 cup butter, softened
1/3 cup honey
3 eggs, well beaten
4 cups wheat flour
1/2 cup raisins
1 teaspoon salt

Directions

1. In a medium bowl, dissolve yeast in warm milk; let stand for 5 minutes.

2. Cream butter and honey in a large bowl with an electric mixer until light and fluffy; add eggs and beat well.

3. Combine flour, salt, and raisins, and add to butter mixture, alternating with milk mixture and beginning and ending with

flour. Mix thoroughly. (Batter will be very stiff.)

4. Cover and let rise until dough has doubled in bulk.
5. Spoon into well-greased tube pan, cover, and let rise until again doubled in bulk.
6. Bake at 350 degrees for 55 minutes. Remove bread from pan and cool on a wire rack.

Cherry Chess Tart
Serves: 6-8

Ingredients
> 1 package prepared pie crust
> 2 eggs
> 1/2 cup sugar
> 2 teaspoons cornmeal
> 1/4 cup buttermilk
> 3 Tablespoons butter, melted
> 2 teaspoons vinegar
> 1 teaspoon vanilla
> 1 21-ounce can cherry pie filling

Directions
1. Prepare pie crust according to package directions for a filled one-crust pie using a 9-inch tart pan.
2. Bake crust at 350 degrees for 5 to 8 minutes.
3. In a medium bowl combine eggs and sugar, mixing well until blended.
4. Add buttermilk, butter, vinegar, and vanilla.
5. Spread cherry pie filling over bottom of prepared pie crust.
6. Pour buttermilk mixture over top of cherry pie filling.
7. Bake at 350 degrees for 50 minutes or until knife inserted in middle of tart comes out clean.

* Cover the outside perimeter of the pie crust with foil to keep it from over-browning.

Packaging Panache

Deliver the food in wicker baskets that have been lined with pretty towels. One of the baskets could be used to hold cards of condolence that arrive in the mail or with flower deliveries. One could be used for addressed thank-you notes ready to be mailed and another for the notes yet to be addressed.

CHAPTER 10

New Pet in Your Home

In wisdom you made them all;
the earth is full of your creatures.
—THE BOOK OF JOB

A passion for pets is one of life's great pleasures. Acquiring a new one is an occasion to "put on the dog," so to speak, with housewarming opportunities for the new addition. The welcoming of this new family member is similar, on a much smaller scale, to the homecoming of a cherished new baby. Whether it is a cat, a dog, a bird, or a potbelly pig, a new pet entering the family will need the proper welcome and paraphernalia to flourish. There are many fun ways to extend your hospitality to a four-legged (or two-legged for our bird buddies) friend.

Love You Can Touch for Adults

Purchase a pet picture frame with the appropriate photos or words describing the pet around the perimeter (like cat or dog). If you are feeling artistic, try taking a regular old frame and painting or stenciling pawprints all around the perimeter of it. Place a gift certificate for obedience school or products at the local pet store in the picture part of the frame. Once the gift certificate is removed, pet lovers can put a prized picture of the new family member in the frame.

All things bright and beautiful,
All creatures great and small,
All things wise and wonderful,
The Lord God made them all.

—Mrs. Alexander

A Christmas ornament with space for a pet picture adds a special touch for a happy holiday.

Love You Can Touch for Children

Help the children start a "Buddy Book" of the family pet. Wrap a little scrapbook in pawprint paper and tuck a roll of film in the bow. Include a stamp of a pawprint and an ink pad so that each page can be decorated with pawprints as the pet owner fills the "Buddy Book" with great pictures.

53

Menu
Buddy's Bone Biscuits (for the family)

*Recipes to Nourish
the Heart and Soul*

Dog bone biscuits make a great housewarming gift to the family welcoming a new puppy. Prepare the 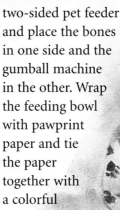 biscuits (these are actually for the family) and write different dog sounds (bow-wow, arf-arf) on each of the biscuits with icing.

Buddy's Bone Biscuits (for the family)
Makes: 2 dozen

Ingredients
3 cups all-purpose flour
1/2 cup dark brown sugar
1/2 teaspoon baking powder
1/2 teaspoon baking soda
1/3 cup honey
2/3 cup water

Directions
1. Preheat oven to 350 degrees.
2. In a large mixing bowl, combine flour, brown sugar, baking powder, and baking soda. Mix on low speed until all ingredients are combined.
3. Add honey and water and mix until combined.
4. Place dough on a lightly floured surface and roll to 1/2-inch thickness.
5. Using a bone-shaped cookie cutter, cut dough. Place bone shapes on a lightly greased cookie sheet.
6. Bake for 15 to 20 minutes, or until browned.

Packaging Panache
A small gumball machine is a perfect container for animal treats. Fill the gumball machine with animal snacks and dispense when needed. Purchase a two-sided pet feeder and place the bones in one side and the gumball machine in the other. Wrap the feeding bowl with pawprint paper and tie the paper together with a colorful dog collar.

54

10 Gift Ideas for the Heart

Personalized Journal—Have a pretty journal monogrammed with your friend's initials.

Unique Glass Bottles—Fill bottles with flavored vinegars and oils, and tie your favorite vinaigrette recipe to the bottleneck.

Set a Pretty Table—Give a gift of eight grapevine wreaths large enough to set dinner plates on. They make for beautiful place-settings.

Colorful Plastic Tote—Fill a big plastic tote with a lid with fun dress-up clothes.

Stocked Picnic Basket—Fill a picnic basket with nonperishable foods.

Hatbox—Fill a hatbox with a classical CD, bubble bath, and a beautiful ceramic cup. Include powdered spice tea and an inspirational poetry book.

Terra-Cotta Pots—Fill pots with flower bulbs, tiny decorative pebbles, garden gloves, and tools.

Glass Carafes—Fill carafes with colorful silk scarves. Put a long straw in the side and top with a white handkerchief.

Favorite Magazine—place a subscription certificate into the pages of your friend's favorite magazine.

Hand-made bookmarks—with inspirational sayings and words of encouragement.

CHAPTER 11

Congratulations

Let's have a feast and celebrate.
—The Book of Luke

A promotion in today's business world is really something to celebrate. A person works hard, waits long, and perseveres under demanding circumstances. Finally, the "Big Brass" notices and a promotion is at hand. It is almost like making it across the finish line in a triathlon, or in the smallest sense of the word, passing "Go" in Monopoly. Succeeding at a job is quite a feat. It is through sheer determination and the power of prayer that anyone makes it to the finish line. Someone who has just made it past the initial securing of a new job needs congratulating, too. A loved one trying to make the right impression in a new job is still under the gun and needs all the support faithful friends and family can dish out.

Love You Can Touch for Adults

During the first few days on a new job, make a huge card for the new employee out of butcher paper. Roll out enough paper to cover the door to his or her home or office. Write in huge letters, "We Are Praying for You!" or "You Can Do It!" Fill in the perimeter of the paper with inspirational verses, quotes, and words of encouragement. Tape the card to the outside or inside of the door, whichever side is most appropriate. This will be a constant reminder that you are offering needed support.

A sorrow shared is but half the trouble but a joy shared is a joy made double!

Another idea is to purchase current magazines that contain pertinent information that your friend or loved one can utilize in his or her job. Or give the person a subscription to a business trade magazine or purchase a computer program that would help the person in his or her new career. Tie magazines up in a big bundle with a colorful plaid ribbon and deliver the stack to his or her home or office.

Love You Can Touch for Children

When new careers are blooming, a child may be receiving less time from his or her parent. You can also give magazine gifts to a child. Find publications that address the child's specific interests and hobbies.

Stack the magazines together and tie up the bundle with a colorful ribbon. If your budget allows, purchase a plastic brief-case and fill it with personal "office supplies" for the child, such as crayons, fun pens, and colorful paper clips.

Menu
Crunching Snow
Dippity Do Da

Recipes to Nourish the Heart and Soul

Crunching Snow
Serves: 6-8

Ingredients
- 1 small box mixed Chex cereal
- 1 cup salted pretzels
- 1 cup peanuts
- 1 cup marshmallows
- 1 cup raisins
- 1 cup dried fruit
- 2 pounds white chocolate, melted

Directions
1. Mix all dry ingredients together in a large mixing bowl.
2. Melt white chocolate in microwave or double boiler. Stir thoroughly until all chocolate is melted.
3. Pour melted white chocolate over dry ingredients.
4. Mix together with clean hands or a large spoon.
5. Spread mixture in a thin layer on wax

paper. When cool, break into small pieces and store in an airtight container.

Dippity Do Da
Makes: 2 dozen

Ingredients
- 2 packages fat pretzel sticks
- 1 pound dark chocolate, melted
- 1 small container silver balls
- 1 small container colored sugar crystals
- 1 small container crushed pistachios

Directions
1. Melt dark chocolate in a double boiler or microwave.
2. Dip ends of pretzels in melted chocolate. Let dry one minute.
3. Pour dipping decorations in a deep small bowl, dip chocolate end of pretzel stick into one of the decorations and place on wax paper. Repeat with other pretzel sticks and decorations.

Packaging Panache

Fill a large decorative tin with a special snacking concoction and attach a note encouraging your friend to take some time to relax with the magazine and snacks and to reflect upon his or her accomplishments. Purchase a unique candy dish and promise to keep it filled with inviting candies for the first month or year in the new job. Also, let your friend or loved one know that you are joining him or her with prayers of praise for her accomplishments and wisdom in every step she takes.

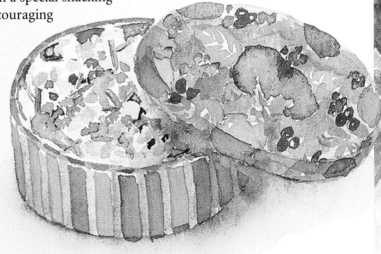

CHAPTER 12

Holidays and Special Days

This is the day the Lord has made; let us rejoice and be glad in it.
—THE BOOK OF PSALMS

Holidays, birthdays, and other special days are all great opportunities to show others how important they are. To tell someone how much you care on these special occasions, take time to find out the person's specific interests and purchase a gift that reflects who they are. A birthday celebration is occasion for balloons or a singing telegram. Always be creative with gift giving. What about something for the person who has everything? A service gift, such as a gift certificate for a facial or a massage works perfectly. Housecleaning services are often appreciated. How about a hot air balloon ride or lunch at a favorite restaurant? Movie passes or video rental coupons are also great gifts. Many men would love a coupon that promises a break from mowing the yard or a gift certificate to a

local hardware store. Gifts can even be as simple as a magazine subscription, a new flavored coffee, or tickets to the zoo. The key to making a special occasion a happy one is knowing the honoree's likes and dislikes. Gift giving should be a pleasure. If you keep that in mind, along with your own budget and time frame, you'll become a master at giving from the heart.

Love You Can Touch for Adults

Purchase a decorative book that contains blank pages. Fill the book with traditional recipes from the generations of your family. On one page, include the recipe, naming it for the relative who makes it or used to prepare it, such as Grandmother Cabaniss' Coconut Pound Cake. On the page opposite the recipe, give a brief biography of that person and your favorite memory or a well-known story involving him or her. Prepare a book like this for each member in your family so that they can each have a special culinary heirloom.

Love is that condition in which the happiness of another person is essential to your own joy.

—Robert A. Heinlin

61

Love You Can Touch for Children

It's a gingerbread man Christmas parade! Prepare several dozen gingerbread men, then wrap them in an airtight plastic bag and freeze. (This reduces the stress level for the parents when decorating day arrives.) When you begin your holiday decorating, set aside one day for decorating gingerbread men for the Christmas parade. Cover your table with wax paper or newspaper and gather up a bunch of festive decorating items. Decorate the cookies, then set them aside to dry. Spray a preserving spray on the gingerbread men and glue hooks on their backs to use as decorations on the tree. (Be sure to make extra cookies for eating! Once sprayed and preserved, they are no longer edible.)

* If the special occasion is not Christmas, have a gingerbread person painting party. Use this as an opportunity to discuss how people are the same on the inside but are all different colors, shapes, and sizes on the outside.

62

Menu
Lemon Pepper Fried Chicken
Smashed Potatoes
Fried Corn Served in the Shuck
Bacon and Onion Green Beans
Sour Cream Biscuits
Birthday Present Cake

*Recipes to Nourish
the Heart and Soul*

Lemon Pepper Fried Chicken
Serves: 4-6

Ingredients
> 8 skinless, boneless chicken breasts
> 1/2 quart buttermilk
> 2 cups flour
> 1 teaspoon salt
> 1 Tablespoon pepper
> 2 Tablespoons fresh lemon zest
> 2 cups Canola oil

Directions
> 1. Soak chicken in buttermilk overnight.
> 2. Combine flour, salt, pepper, and lemon

zest in a large resealable bag.
3. Place chicken in the flour mixture and shake thoroughly to coat. Remove and shake off excess flour.
4. Place oil in a large skillet and heat to 350 degrees. Fry chicken breasts a few at a time for 12 to 15 minutes, turning every 4 minutes. When batter becomes a deep golden color, remove from pan and drain off excess oil.

* If you are packaging chicken in a hat box, be sure it is cooled so that it will not be soggy. Then place it in a plastic bag so the grease will not get on the hat box.

Smashed Potatoes
Serves: 4

Ingredients
> 6 large potatoes
> 4 Tablespoons butter
> salt and pepper to taste

Grown-ups
> 1 Tablespoon horseradish
> 1 teaspoon garlic

Directions
> 1. Wash, peel, and cube potatoes.
> 2. Fill a large saucepan with water and bring to a boil.
> 3. Place potatoes in boiling water and boil

until fork-tender.

4. When potatoes are fork-tender, beat with electric mixer until smooth.
5. Add butter and stir to combine. Add salt and pepper to taste.
6. Set aside some potatoes for the kids, stir in the grown-up ingredients, and mix to combine.

Fried Corn Served in the Shuck
Serves: 4

Ingredients

1 pound frozen corn (or corn cut off the cob)
2 Tablespoons butter
salt and pepper to taste

Directions

1. Place butter in skillet and melt.
2. Add corn and fry until thoroughly warmed. Season with salt and pepper.
3. Serve in washed corn husks.

Bacon and Onion Green Beans
Serves: 4

Ingredients

1 pound fresh green beans
2 slices peppered bacon
1 small onion, sliced
salt and pepper to taste

Directions

1. Place peppered bacon in a large skillet and cook for 3 minutes. Add sliced onion and continue to cook until onion is soft.
2. Add green beans and stir to coat with bacon drippings. Cover skillet with lid and steam for 5 minutes.

Sour Cream Biscuits
Makes: 1 dozen

Ingredients

2 cups biscuit mix
1 stick butter, melted
1 cup sour cream
1/2 cup Cheddar cheese, grated

Directions

1. Place biscuit mix in a medium bowl and add melted butter.
2. Stir in sour cream and cheese.
3. Spray muffin tin with cooking spray.
4. Spoon biscuit batter into muffin tin, filling the sections half-full.
5. Bake for 10 to 12 minutes or until golden brown.

Birthday Present Cake
Makes: 1 large cake

Ingredients
　　2 packaged layer cake mixes
　　frosting
　　ribbon and bow
　　fresh flowers

Directions
　　1. Prepare cake according to package directions. After preparing both cake mixes you should have 4 layers of cake. Frost and stack the four layers as usual.
　　2. Measure the height of the cake to figure the length of ribbon you need to go over the cake in two directions. Make a plus sign on the top of the cake with the ribbon. Top the cake with a large bow. Place small fresh flowers in the large bow and you have a present that looks pretty and will taste delicious.

Packaging Panache

Find three decorative boxes in graduated sizes; hatboxes work great for this. Choose a recipe from your collection that will fit in one of your boxes and prepare it. Place the other menu items in the largest hatbox. Gather photographs of the person from birth to present day in a mini photo album. Last, include your book of recipes with a bookmark to indicate the page where the dishes you prepared are featured. Place those items in the smallest hatbox. Stack the boxes largest to smallest and cover with colored cellophane. Secure the wrap at the top with a big bow.

Fabulous Food Finds

Simple food gifts are always a welcome sight, whether given as a hostess gift or as a small Christmas remembrance for a special teacher. Here are some ideas that can be made in advance.

1/2 cup brown sugar
1/4 cup orange juice concentrate
1 Tablespoon orange rind, grated
1/2 cup favorite nuts, chopped

Directions
Place all ingredients except nuts in a medium saucepan. Cook until cranberries pop, stirring occasionally. Add nuts and store in clean canning jars. Serve with grilled meats or roasted turkey.

Super-Sensational Salsa
Makes: 1 cup

Ingredients
1 yellow onion, finely chopped
4 Roma tomatoes, finely chopped
1/4 cup cilantro, finely chopped
1/2 cup spicy tomato juice

Holiday or Everyday Chutney
Yield: 2 cups

Ingredients
2 cups fresh cranberries
1 cup Granny Smith apples, peeled and chopped

1 Tablespoon oil
1 Tablespoon jalapeños, finely
    chopped
2 Tablespoons red wine vinegar
1 Tablespoon balsamic vinegar
1 whole clove garlic, finely chopped
salt and pepper to taste

Directions

Combine all ingredients in a clear jar. Place the lid on tightly and shake to combine. Chill overnight.

*Serve with tortilla chips, chicken, tacos, or tortilla-wrapped scrambled eggs.

Simple-and-Fancy Shortbread
Makes: 1 dozen

Ingredients

1/2 pound butter
1/2 cup sugar
1 teaspoon vanilla extract
1 teaspoon almond extract
2 cups flour

Directions

1. Preheat oven to 300 degrees.

2. Cream ingredients together. Knead for a few minutes and place in a 9 x 9-inch pan.
3. Smooth dough with bottom of a glass to flatten. Bake for 45 to 50 minutes or until golden brown.
4. Cut bars while still hot, but leave in pan to cool.

Once the shortbread has cooled, dip one end into melted chocolate and then into coconut, crushed pistachios, or roasted almonds.

Chocolate Pretzels
Makes: 10 servings

Ingredients

1 bag of pretzel knots
2 cups chocolate, melted

Directions

1. Place pretzels in a large mixing bowl. Pour melted chocolate over pretzels and stir to combine.
2. Set chocolate-covered pretzels on wax paper to dry.

While pretzels are drying, shake colorful sprinkles over them. After the chocolate has dried, melt a little white chocolate and drizzle it over the chocolate-covered pretzels.

In the Dough (cookie mix in a jar)
Makes: 2 dozen

Assemble the first nine ingredients in a quart jar from top to bottom. Top with a decorative piece of cloth and the jar lid. Write the recipe on a small card and tie it to the top of the jar. (The recipient will add the other ingredients.)

Ingredients

   1 cup chocolate chips
   1/2 cup brown sugar
   3/4 cup sugar
   1 1/4 cup oatmeal
   1 cup flour
   1/2 teaspoon baking powder
   1/2 teaspoon baking soda
   1/4 teaspoon salt
   1/2 cup butter
   (recipient adds the following
       ingredients:)
   1 egg
   1 1/2 teaspoon vanilla extract
   1/2 teaspoon almond extract

Directions

   1. Cream the butter and sugars. Add dry ingredients and stir to combine. Fold in chocolate chips.
   2. Bake at 375 degrees for 9 to 12 minutes.

Quick Chocolate Truffles
Makes: 2 dozen

Ingredients

   1/2 cup evaporated milk
   1/4 cup sugar
   2 cups milk chocolate chips
   1 teaspoon almond extract
   1 cup toasted almonds, finely chopped

Directions

   1. Combine milk and sugar in a heavy saucepan. Cook over medium heat until mixture comes to a full boil. Boil 3 minutes, stirring constantly.
   2. Remove from heat and stir in chocolate chips and extract. Chill for 45 minutes.
   3. Roll into 1-inch balls, then roll in almonds and set in candy paper cups. Chill until ready to serve.

You can replace the almond extract with vanilla or liqueurs such as Frangelico, Créme de menthe, Chambord, or Grand Marnier.

CHAPTER 13

Divorce

A friend loves at all times, and a brother is born for adversity.
—The Book of Proverbs

Only those who have experienced a divorce can fully understand the magnitude of pain involved. Offering sympathy and support without taking sides is the best approach. It's important to focus on the friend personally, not the circumstances or events leading up to the divorce. It is also important to do things to help this person feel special. No spoken words can take away the pain that is the result of a broken marriage. Acknowledging a friend's loss instead of ignoring the problem makes all the difference and shows them that they are not alone. You can't go wrong with words that are simple, true, and from the heart.

Love You Can Touch for Adults

Prepare a scone, tea, and china basket. Select your friend's favorite tea. Find uplifting verses and quotes and type them or write them on decorative paper. Cut the paper into small enough sizes to be stapled to the end of the string on a tea bag. Put each tea bag back into the box and tie a beautiful ribbon around it.

> *Sometimes the very kindest deed we can do is just to listen when a neighbor needs someone to talk to; other times we need to express our love in actions.*
>
> —Edwina Patterson

Love You Can Touch for Children

At this traumatic time in a child's life, it is vital that he or she feels the love and care of others. So many emotions run rampant while this child's little world is totally rearranged. Try putting together a "You're the Best" box. Purchase a heart-shaped box and fill it with heart-shaped items— stickers, stamps, candy, paperweights, soap, little storybooks about love and friendship. Place a note in the box that says, "Your mommy and daddy really love you, and so do I." You might want to include a book for children that talks about divorce. (I recommend *Divorce Happens to the Nicest Kids* by Michael Prokop, published by Alegra House.)

Menu
Dried Peach Scones
Assorted Teas

*Recipes to Nourish
the Heart and Soul*

Dried Peach Scones
Makes: 1 dozen

Ingredients
>   1 1/2 cups flour
>   1/2 cup rolled oats
>   1/2 cup sugar
>   1/2 cup dried peaches, chopped
>   1 Tablespoon baking powder
>   1/2 teaspoon baking soda
>   1/2 teaspoon salt
>   1 teaspoon cinnamon
>   1/2 cup buttermilk
>   1/3 cup unsalted butter, melted
>   1 large egg

Glaze
>   1 large egg
>   1 teaspoon water

Directions
1. Preheat oven to 375 degrees. Butter baking sheet, set aside.
2. Put flour, oats, sugar, peaches, baking powder, baking soda, salt, and cinnamon in mixing bowl. Stir to combine.
3. Mix buttermilk, butter, and egg in a small dish. Add to the flour mixture. Stir just until moistened; dough will be in clumps. Do not overmix.
4. Form the dough into a ball; dough will be moist. Turn dough onto a well-floured board and knead until it holds together and is smooth. Pat dough into a circle about 3/8-inch thick. Cut into scone shapes using a round cookie cutter. Place scones about 2 inches apart on the prepared baking sheet.
5. In a small bowl mix together egg and water. Brush mixture lightly over top of scones. Bake about 15 minutes or until tops are lightly golden.

Packaging Panache

Place your gift items in a pretty wicker basket lined with two floral napkins and tied with coordinating ribbon. Purchase two inexpensive china teacups and saucers and prepare some dried peach scones. Wrap the scones in colored plastic wrap and place them in large Chinese food containers. If your budget allows, a CD of classical piano music makes a lovely finishing touch. Wrap the basket in matching colored plastic wrap and tie with a ribbon. Use the same decorative paper you used for the verses and quotes on the tea bags to write a note suggesting a time the two of you could visit for a cup of tea and conversation.

CHAPTER 14

Someone Special Going on a Trip

May the Lord keep watch between you and me when we are away from each other.
—THE BOOK OF GENESIS

Just taking the opportunity to get away provides a new lease on life. A good trip gives a person a chance to put priorities in perspective and recharge his or her batteries. It is especially nice to travel to a place with beautifully scenic surroundings. It serves as a powerful reminder of the wonder of creation. Traveling can be a bit intimidating when the surroundings are new and the language is foreign. If someone has traveled to a place their friends have yet to see they have the perfect opportunity to share their favorites in food, shopping, and fun. Here are a few helpful suggestions for maximizing a loved one's vacation.

Love You Can Touch for Adults

Fodor's travel books offer a great look at a new city or country. They highlight the best restaurants, activities, and must-sees for the traveler. Enclose a gift certificate for an interesting-sounding restaurant inside your friend's "favorite things" area in the book. Wrap the book with a map of that city or country and you have contributed to an exciting getaway.

If the vacationers already have travel books, give them a lead-lined container for vacation film so it will be protected from airport x-ray machines.

The heart turns to travel...

—Ezra Pound

Love You Can Touch for Children

Activity books rolled, tied and placed in a little book bag will help time pass quickly as young traveler's wait in a car, airport, or train station. Travel treats are also a welcome sight for both parents and children.

Recipes to Nourish the Heart and Soul

Crunchy munchies are a must for a traveling brigade. A wooden cheese box full of crunchy vegetables, fruits, and crackers will help hunger pangs subside. This is really a "grocery store trip" menu. Use plastic bags to make these snacks portable.

Garden Vegetables and More

Ingredients
- carrots
- cauliflower
- broccoli
- asparagus
- eggplant
- apples
- pears
- assortment of dried fruits
- miniature crackers
- small bread sticks
- pretzels
- breath mints

Little Dippers

Ingredients
- Store-bought dips: creamy blue cheese, French onion, pimento cheese, strawberry cream cheese, sour cream with brown sugar
- small reusable ice pack

Packaging Panache

Line the lid of a small plastic tote with mini ice packs and top with a small vinyl tablecloth. Put the dips in first so they will remain chilled, then place fruits, vegetables, and crackers inside. Package the crackers in colored plastic wrap and tie them in small bundles, or just place the entire box of crackers in the tote. To help with clean-up, include antibacterial hand gel, moist wipes, and napkins.

10 Ideas for Tuck'n Love into Your Husband's Lunchbox

Favorite Team Schedule—If your husband is a sports guy, a game schedule from his favorite team would be a great little item to add to his lunch.

Handmade Paperweight—Homemade playdough will harden when baked. Make a batch and then form a heart shape. Put the imprint of your child's hand in the center. Place a special "I Love You" message in with the gift.

Tee for Two—Schedule a golf date. Include a little note that details the time and the place.

CD or Cassette Tape—Music can smooth the rough edges of a hectic day at the office. Tuck in a favorite CD or cassette for a "We Are Thinking of You" message.

Petite Box of Chocolates—My husband is a chocolate lover, so a petite box of designer chocolates with gooey centers is always a special treat.

Hero Star—Purchase a big heart sticker and write on the sticker, "You're Our Hero."

You're Our HERO!

Cartoon Clippings—Funny cartoon clippings can really lift a harried spirit. Try finding a favorite and including it in his lunch.

Sporting Event Tickets—Place tickets to a favorite sporting event in a sandwich bag.

Picnic Note—Place a note in his lunchbox inviting him to join the family for a picnic in a beautiful park after work.

DADDY

Children's Art—Have an art time with the kids and ask them to create a picture for Daddy's office. Roll up the picture and tie it with a pretty plaid ribbon.

CHAPTER 15

Celebrating Children

Let the little children come to me, and do not hinder them,
for the Kingdom of God belongs to such as these.
—THE BOOK OF LUKE

Celebrating children and spending "good" time together, where the entire focus is on the child, offers both parents and children a chance to play. It also gives busy people the opportunity to relax with friends and enjoy one another's families. Sometimes in order to really get to know and understand their children, parents need to get away with them. At home, the phone rings, the laundry needs washing, the groceries need to be bought and the meals cooked. A getaway time lets people be themselves without a big list of to-do's. Adults really can be children again as they watch, play, and learn with their children. The children can play, love, and respond to parents who are not harried. This picnic will help parents rediscover the child in them who has been kept from play because of the demands of being an adult.

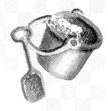

Love You Can Touch for Adults

As a unique twist on everyday entertaining, invite some families to join you at the lake or at a beautiful park in your community. Make your party a brunch on a crisp Saturday morning. Plan a menu that includes great to-go foods. As a gift for your friends, write the recipes in a pretty book entitled "Recipes from Friends" and present it to them during dessert.

> *Do not be afraid of showing your affection. Be warm and tender, thoughtful and affectionate.*
>
> —JOHN LUBBOCK

Love You Can Touch for Children

Provide special outdoor games to maximize playtime. You might try having a dads-and-kids game time so the moms can have the opportunity to catch up on conversation, then reverse the game time so the dads can have their social time, too. You could also include a fun childrens recipe in the "Recipes from Friends" book to help them remember the enjoyable occasion.

Menu
Waffle Sandwiches
Breakfast Balls
Cookout Banana Splits
Hot Coffee, Chilled Juices, and Bottled Waters

Recipes to Nourish the Heart and Soul

Waffle Sandwiches
Serves: 3

Ingredients
> 6 round frozen waffles
> 4 Tablespoons strawberry jam
> 2 Tablespoons cream cheese, softened
> 4 slices bacon, crisply fried and crumbled
> fresh strawberries

Directions
> 1. Prepare waffles in toaster according to package directions.

2. In a small bowl combine jam, cream cheese, and crumbled bacon.
3. Spread one side of waffle with cream cheese and bacon mixture. Top with fresh strawberries and a second waffle to make a sandwich.

* If you are taking this menu to the park, most pavilion areas are equipped with electricity. Go ahead and bring the toaster and prepare these at the park. If electricity is not available, prepare without the strawberries and wrap tightly with foil. Bring strawberries separately and place them on waffles before serving.

Breakfast Balls
Serves: 6-8

Ingredients
> 1/2 pound ground turkey sausage
> 4 eggs, scrambled
> 2 8-count packages of crescent roll dough
> 1/2 cup Cheddar cheese, grated

Directions
> 1. In a skillet brown sausage, drain and pat with paper towels to get rid of excess grease. Set aside in a covered plate to keep warm.
> 2. Place eggs in same skillet and scramble until firm.
> 3. Place sausage and eggs back in skillet to warm, sprinkle with cheese.

4. Remove crescent roll dough from package and spread each piece on a sheet of waxed paper.
5. Place one spoonful of egg and sausage mixture into center of each piece of dough.
6. Roll dough into a ball and place on a cookie sheet. Bake according to package directions. If taking to the park, wrap tightly with foil and place in a warming pouch.

Cookout Banana Splits
Serves: 4-6

Ingredients
>   4 to 6 bananas
>   1/2 cup peanut butter
>   1/2 cup mini marshmallows
>   1/2 cup mini chocolate morsels
>   Maraschino cherries

Directions
1. Peel bananas, slicing most of the way lengthwise and leaving bottoms attached.
2. Spread insides of bananas with peanut butter.
3. Sprinkle with mini marshmallows and mini chocolate morsels.
4. Wrap each banana in aluminum foil and place it on fire or grill until marshmallows and chocolate melt.
5. Top with cherries to serve.

* Add a big basket of seasonal fruits, a small knife and cutting board, a selection of gourmet cheeses and cookies, and a few fruit muffins. Include a big thermos of coffee, small bottles of chilled juices, and bottled waters.

Packaging Panache
Place the food items in tote bags, backpacks, plastic storage boxes, or wicker picnic baskets. Wrap the different containers in colorful large sheets, old quilts, or beach towels and tie with heavy twine. Once you arrive at your picnic location, toss the container wrappings on the ground and use them as a comfortable place to relax.

Life is made up not of great sacrifices or duties, but
of little things, in which smiles and kindnesses and
small obligations, given habitually, are what win and
preserve the heart and secure comfort.

Sɪʀ H. Dᴀᴠʏ